SELF CULTURE

A COURSE OF LESSONS ON
DEVELOPING THE PHYSICAL
UNFOLDING THE SOUL & AT-
TAINING UNTO *The* SPIRITUAL

By LEVI

Transcriber of
THE AQUARIAN GOSPEL
of
JESUS THE CHRIST

E. S. DOWLING, Publisher
Los Angeles, California
1912

♣

FOR SALE BY
E. S. DOWLING
Los Angeles, California

Kessinger Publishing's
Rare Mystical Reprints

THOUSANDS OF SCARCE BOOKS ON THESE AND OTHER SUBJECTS:

Freemasonry * Akashic * Alchemy * Alternative Health * Ancient Civilizations * Anthroposophy * Astrology * Astronomy * Aura * Bible Study * Cabalah * Cartomancy * Chakras * Clairvoyance * Comparative Religions * Divination * Druids * Eastern Thought * Egyptology * Esoterism * Essenes * Etheric * ESP * Gnosticism * Great White Brotherhood * Hermetics * Kabalah * Karma * Knights Templar * Kundalini * Magic * Meditation * Mediumship * Mesmerism * Metaphysics * Mithraism * Mystery Schools * Mysticism * Mythology * Numerology * Occultism * Palmistry * Pantheism * Parapsychology * Philosophy * Prosperity * Psychokinesis * Psychology * Pyramids * Qabalah * Reincarnation * Rosicrucian * Sacred Geometry * Secret Rituals * Secret Societies * Spiritism * Symbolism * Tarot * Telepathy * Theosophy * Transcendentalism * Upanishads * Vedanta * Wisdom * Yoga * *Plus Much More!*

DOWNLOAD A FREE CATALOG
AND
SEARCH OUR TITLES AT:

www.kessinger.net

Copyright 1912, by
E. S. DOWLING
Copyright in England, 1912
Entered at Stationer's Hall, London

ALL RIGHTS RESERVED
Including Rights of Translation

CONTENTS

LESSON		PAGE
I.	Practical Methods of Developing Thought Power. The Selfs	5
II.	A Retentive Memory for Everyday. Practical Studies in How to Remember	17
III.	Colors, Nature's Medicines and Beautifiers. What Colors to Wear to be Attractive and Healthful	31
IV.	The Secret of Popularity and Leadership. Short Cuts to Personal Magnetism	43
V.	Unfolding the Powers of the Soul	57
VI.	The Helpfullness of Unseen Forces in Individual Unfoldment; Magical Operations	69
VII.	The Holy Spirit. The Holy Ghost of Modern Theology as a Myth and a Feality. Its Identity the Secret of Jesus. Its Reception the Culmination of Spiritual Unfoldment	81

SELF CULTURE
PRACTICAL METHODS OF DEVELOPING THOUGHT POWER

LESSON I.
THE SELFS.

This Course of Instruction on Self Culture is intended to cover all the requirements of the perfect man, and it seems well in the outset to make a critical inquiry into the meaning of the word Self.

When Elizabeth, the mother of John the Baptist, and Mary, the mother of Jesus, were pupils in the Esoteric School of Elihu and Salome in the city of Zoan in Egypt, Elihu taught them a lesson that is truly remarkable in its clearness and conciseness of expression. I will repeat it as a basic Postulate.

The Lesson of Elihu, "There are two selfs; the higher and the lower self.

"The higher self is human spirit clothed with soul, made in the form of God.

"The lower self, the carnal self, the body of desires, is a reflection of the higher self, distorted by the murky ethers of the flesh.

"The lower self is an illusion, and will pass away; the higher self is God in man, and will not pass away.

"The higher self is the embodiment of truth; the lower self is truth reversed, and so, is falsehood manifest.

"The higher self is justice, mercy, love and right; the lower self is what the higher self is not.

"The lower self breeds hatred, slander, lewdness, murders, theft, and everything that harms; the higher self is mother of the virtues and the harmonies of life.

"The lower self is rich in promises, but poor in blessedness and peace; it offers pleasure, joy and satisfying gains; but gives unrest and misery and death.

"It gives men apples that are lovely to the eye and pleasant to the smell; their cores are full of bitterness and gall.

"If you would ask me what to study I would say, yourselfs; and when you well had studied them, and then would ask me what to study next, I would reply, yourselfs.

"He who well knows his lower self, knows the illusions of the world, knows of the things that pass away; and he who knows his higher self, knows God; knows well the things that cannot pass away.

"Thrice blessed is the man who has made purity and love his very own; he has been ransomed from the perils of the lower self and is himself his higher self." Aquarian Gospel, chapter 8.

Personality and Individuality. These two words are often used interchangeably, as though they meant one and the same thing, when in truth they differ widely in signification. The personality is the lower self; the Individuality is the higher self. Put in more comprehensive language: the Personality is the physical body with its eccentricities and its senses; the Individuality is the soul with its characteristics and its senses. We **develop** the Personality: we **unfold** the Individuality.

Of course these are so intimately connected that while we are in the body it is difficult to consider them separately, because the body and its functions are but exponents of the soul and its characteristics. Example: Intelligence is an attribute of soul; Intellection is a function of the physical organism. The Intellect is really the organ through which Intelligence is manifest.

Intelligence, per se, is a universal ether pervading all space; the Intellect is a machine that seizes these ethers, concentrates them and makes them serve the lower self and all manifest things. The lower self is, in fact, the connection between the psychic world and the world of manifests; so while we tabernacle here in the flesh we must recognize the value of the lower self, restrain its carnality and develop that which is needful in psychic and spiritual unfoldment.

The Physical Body is the Temple of the Holy Breath and it is the manifest abiding place of the soul. Paul had a clear conception of this idea when he wrote to the disciples at Corinth: "Know ye not that ye are the Temple of God, and that the Spirit of God dwelleth in you?

"If any man defile the Temple of God, him will God destroy, (that is, this particular Temple because of its defilement will disintegrate, die), for the Temple of God must be holy, which Temple ye are." I. Cor. 3:16, 17.

The Care of the Physical Body is of paramount importance and this course of Self Culture will cover in detail the most approved methods of Self Healing and of developing every part of the body, including the intellectual faculties, the memory and the senses.

Self Culture carries one beyond the development of the **Personality** into the domain of the higher self, and comprises the most approved methods of Psychic and Spiritual unfoldment, which, likewise, will be covered in this Course of Instruction.

Thought-Power lies at the foundation of all culture, and our very first work must be to develop that power, and this lesson is to be devoted largely to the most practical methods of making thought powerful.

What Is It To Think? It is to keep the machinery of the Intellect in motion so that the ethers of Intelligence, which are everywhere present, may be concentrated, formed into ideas. There are two kinds of thinking: **Voluntary** and **Involuntary**. Some people find the mechanism of Thought feebly running soon after birth, and they just let it continue to run, directed by whatever influences happen to surround them. They make no effort to change the trend of thought, nor to make it more powerful. These people are **Involuntary Thinkers**; they are thought automatons; they are contented to follow in the wake of ancestors and early teachers. They are creatures of circumstance and have no faith whatever in the Powers of Thought to control anything. They are firm believers in luck, and when things go awry they say, "It is just my luck." If they are successful in anything they call it, "A streak of good luck."

Voluntary Thinkers are those whose **wills** are practical engineers, and are able to control the machinery of thought. Mark, there is a world of difference between the conditions of persons who are controlled by machines, and those who control the machines. This not being a lesson on Theory we cannot here make a study of the Will and its place in the dual man. We are now looking for practical things and men have long since learned that Will controls destiny, and is the arbitrator of Luck; so we assume that you are sufficiently versed in the philosophy of the Intellect to recognize the fact that Will is the true power behind the throne in all matters pertaining to the selfs.

How to Develop Will-Power is of first importance in this study of the development of Thought-Power.

Will and Desire must not be confounded. Desire springs from the heart-side of things. Desire belongs to the lower self wholly; personal satisfaction is the inspiration of desires. I love, and I have an intense desire to be with and serve my loved ones; this is a source of personal gratification. In the domain of the higher self, desires are in abeyance.

The body of desires, of which we will speak later on, must be disintegrated before one can enter the realms of true spiritual consciousness. In this work of evolvement Will must be absolute Lord of desires. It is, therefore, evident that the student must first learn how to strengthen the powers of Will. The poet gave us more than an intimation of the philosophy of Attainment when he wrote: "We rise by the things that are under our feet." When we come to recognize the full significance of this truism we find that we must reverse the current order of thought, for we have been taught in school, family, church and Sunday school that we gain heaven by our **virtues;** but our virtues ought never to be under our feet. The advancing Neophite firmly plants his feet upon his Vices, and so rises into the light of God, and so we are brought face to face with the fact that there is some good in our Vices, for we rise by the things that are under our feet.

A Study of Vices is in place at this juncture. Every man, woman and child is a householder, and has a large herd of unclean animals in his pasture. A good Astral seer can see these animals as they continually follow the householder about, and there is always a great, big, many-headed monster who is nearest to him. In unembellished language, these monsters are his vices, and everybody has one vice considerably larger than any of the rest. Paul calls this one, "The sin that doth most easily beset us." Let every one pause for a moment and take a peep into the pastures of the heart, and view his family of devils, little and big, and see if he cannot name the big fellow who continually dogs his steps like a shadow of the night. What is your principal vice?

Strengthening the Will is the immediate object of this study, and with this host of heliomonsters to be destroyed we certainly have opportunities for effort. Nothing is ever strengthened by inertia. Activity and nothing else, will make strong a muscle, an organ, a faculty; so in order to strengthen the Will, an enemy and a battle ground must be found; for every advance must be made by antagonisms.

In the first round, what is the antagonist of Will? Her name is Desire. This is the family name. The family is large, and every child a lusty fellow. Note the names in the

Directory: Lust-Desire, Theft-Desire, Envy-Desire, Revenge-Desire, Greed-Desire, Jealous-Desire, Slander-Desire, Tobacco-Desire, Alcohol-Desire, Trouble-Desire—but the Directory is too full of names for all to be mentioned. The Will has just let these children grow and every one is now a master.

Mark, the Will is weak, and no matter what the resolution may be, the Will cannot down all these enemies at one fell stroke; and, furthermore, the captain of the host is too powerful to be attacked at first. I have known men whose greatest foe was the liquor habit, or the morphine habit, or tobacco habit, to enter into a solemn agreement with themselves that they would throttle the monster, and they began the fight well but their Wills were too weak and the monster came out the victor, and the poor fellows sank down into deeper sloughs of despondency. They simply tried too much at first.

You well know the results of continuous failure. The marshy grounds of discouragements are nearby. But when people catch the contagion of Aspiration they are apt to attempt the conquest of everything in sight all at once and, to use an American phrase, "They fall down." American people in particular are extremists. You are apt to find them well up toward the top of the mountain, or lying in the muddy slough of despair. If they cannot be great oaks or tall sycamores they are apt to be skunk cabbages, or rushes growing up from quagmires or stagnant pools.

It is hard indeed for people to learn that an oak does not attain unto its majority in a day. Substantial growth makes haste slowly. Reformations that are solid to the core are never instantaneous. They may manifest themselves all at once, as was the case in the conversion of the Christian Apostle Paul. Perhaps most people can call to mind instances of so-called miraculous conversions, when a veritable devil became a saint in a night. And some of these conversions (a very few of them) are genuine. In all these instances, however, men see only results. The leaven had been working for years. The divine plant had been growing under a cover for a long time and some master-hand succeeded in lifting the lid, and the full-fledged convert pops out like Jack from a magic box.

The Process of Will-strengthening is not a rapid one, and the student must not try to force the growth in a day. One should not attempt to throttle the **great** demon of his life the moment he is awakened to moral consciousness. He should try his Will on little things.

The Tree of Desire is not an ordinary shurb. It is a deadly Upas tree, and grows like the great Banyan tree of India and the West India Isles. One center stock shoots up from the soil and when it has attained a height of from 20 to 80 feet it throws out immense branches which bend to the earth, the tips of which take root and grow; so every tree has many offsprings, and while each shoot originates in the Parent tree and ever holds its relationship with the center tree, it nourishes itself from the soil. Likewise the Desire Tree of every person is a unit, is one from which every other desire springs. He who can analyze himself and know the name and character of the great stock of his Desire Tree has done something toward its destruction; but he must know that all his lesser evils spring from the parent evil; but like the branches of the great Banyan tree, every branch or sin bent to the earth takes root and may have an independent existence.

The Character of the Parent Tree is the character of the Person.

Avarice may be the name of the Parent tree; if so we have an avaricious person, and every sin of his life springs from, and takes on the complexion of the parent.

Lust may be the name of the parent tree; if so, every action of the life is steeped in lust and all the offshoots are lustful and the man's chief desire is to gratify lust.

Selfishness is the name of a great majority of the stocks of Desire from which all evils spring. Every thing that a selfish person does can be traced directly to the great desire for selfish gratification. He who is a good student of motives, can tell by the acts of a person the name and character of his parent Desire Tree.

In Will-Strengthening one must begin and

destroy these hideous children, for while springing from the parent, each has become an independent tree. Mystic brethren and sisters, take your ax from the Lodge Room, sharpen it up and go to work on the little trees that have originated in your great Upas Tree of sin. These are the little foxes that spoil the vines, of which a Hebrew prophet wrote.

Your Will may now be strong enough to overcome what seems to be a little sin, like evil speaking, harshness in word and deed, ungratefulness, egotism, self importance, self righteousness, etc. One such evil over come by sheer force of Will, and the Will is strengthened so that other evils may be destroyed, and, by and by, the great Upas Tree itself may be dominated by Will.

The Weakest People we meet are the ones who believe their Wills are strong, but are afraid of putting them to the test. Men and women are plentiful who tell us that their habits are under the control of the Will. These people are apt to assert, "I can quit smoking, or chewing tobacco, drinking booze, tea or coffee, taking morphine, visiting vile dives of corruption, gambling, etc., whenever I please." These are all hot-house plants, and are the weakest creatures on earth. They haven't Will power enough to be truly respectable when invited into our parlors and drawing rooms. In an experience of many years in aggressive temperance work I have met hundreds of men and women who insisted that they could quit drinking if they wanted to; but not one per cent of the entire outfit ever did quit. "Let him who thinketh he standeth take heed lest he fall."

He who can control his personal desires, has his Thought-machinery under control, and can easily make the elements of the earth, the water, the fire and the air come and go at his bidding.

LESSON II.

A RETENTIVE MEMORY FOR EVERYBODY—PRACTICAL STUDIES IN HOW TO REMEMBER

A good memory is a wonderful accomplishment; when one possesses such he readily accumulates knowledge; when one has a poor memory he is handicapped at every turn of life's intellectual highway. It is evident, then, that in this course of lessons in **Self Culture** we should make a careful study of the best methods of developing this mental capacity.

Memory is the faculty registering impressions and thought-concepts upon certain sensitized films of the brain.

Recollection is the faculty of reproducing, bringing to objective consciousness, the registered impressions and thought-concepts.

A Good Memory registers impressions and concepts with sufficient power to make the record indelible.

A Poor Memory registers them in such a superficial manner that they cannot be readily reproduced.

Memorizing; By this we mean the processes of registering impressions or thought-concepts. We may well recognize two processes of memorizing.

Involuntary; this word quite well indicates the character of the first process. Some teachers call this process Sensuous memory, because the memorizing is effected by and through the senses. We see scenes, hear sounds, taste flavors, smell odors and feel sensations without the will acting in any perceptible manner; but these sense-functions make indelible impressions upon the sensitized films of the brain, and sometimes there is so much power back of the sensations that they may be re-called, or may come without any effort of the Will to recall, at any time. Such memorizing may be automatic.

This involuntary memorizing may be carried further than the reception of impressions through the senses; for there is such a thing as

Involuntary Thinking. All space is surcharged with the atoms of thought, and every sort of an intellect automatically, involuntarily, makes use of some of them; so, some concepts are registered upon the brain films without the action of the Will.

These two processes cover the ground suggested by the caption, Involuntary Memorizing. These automatic memorizers may find their impressions to be so powerful that they may be greatly annoyed, even made frantic by the vividness of their recollections. A simpleton may be frightened to death by the involuntary recollections of past events.

Voluntary Memorizing is the Second Process to be Considered. This process may be improved and this lesson will be devoted to the "How to do it." **Poor Memorizers** are everywhere in evidence. It is no especial disgrace to be born with a poor memory, but it is a disgrace to keep one. Many people seem to be contented to heap all their spiritual, and moral, and intellectual imperfections upon a poor memory. They will not enter into the deeper studies of Occultism because they "cannot remember;" these people do not seem to understand that in these days of universal opportunities, it is a shame and a disgrace for one to continue to have a poor memory.

It might be interesting for us to make a study of the **cause** of poor memories; but as there could be no helpful results from such a study we dismiss the theme, and begin with the acknowledged fact that most people have aggravated symptoms of poor memories.

The Three-Fold Character of Voluntary Memorizing may here be considered. The senses may be strengthened by the potentized habit of accurate observation, so that external impressions that ordinarily are not recognized, may be recorded on the brain-film in a lasting manner. An **automatic** observer will pass along the streets of our city and sense only such things as appeal to his idiosyncrasies, while a cultured observer will sense everything. This potentized habit of accurate observation makes the voluntary memorizer strong in **Sensuous Memory.**

Intellectual Process of Memorizing is the second and higher stage of memory. This brings one in touch with the soul of things. All manifests are but results of thought-concepts, and the educated thinker is constantly in contact with the real, or the things that the physical senses cannot recognize, and does not need to receive sensuous or illusive impressions.

Thought in action, and dealing largely with the soul-side of things, intensifies the power of the memory. The man who **thinks** in a systematic manner becomes a giant in memorizing.

Inspiration is the highest process of developing the memory. This is the only process that is truly Occult. The atmosphere is charged with a purifying ether that has the power of disintegrating the resistance molecules that render the brain-films non-receptive.

To make use of this process the student must be somewhat familiar with what the Orientalists call the Yoga of Discrimination; know how to call to his assistance just what he needs, being well assured that Will is master of the ethers, and that they will respond when conditions make it possible for them to do so.

Without now entering into a critical study of the Hindu Viveka we may give a single exercise that will well cover the helpfulness of the process of Inspiration.

Exercise: Assume an easy position and by somewhat vigorous breathing, throw out of the body what may with some propriety be called "the dead breath;" then concentrate your thought upon the specific ether, the spiritual ether of purification, and with this thought uppermost slowly inspire through the nostrils until the lungs, yea, the whole body, is filled with the breath; and this is the Holy Breath, the purifying breath of the Spirit.

If this exercise is taken properly you will feel a tingling sensation in all parts of the body; the brain will become clear as a bell, the memory films will be cleansed, and you will, with a single effort, realize that there is much more in divine inspiration, or inspiring the superfine ethers, than you have ever thought.

The Three Processes of Improving the Memory must be kept in mind:

1. Potentized habit of accurate observation;
2. Systematic, concentrative thinking;
3. Inspiration, or taking in the purifying ethers.

Attention lies at the foundation of every process of memory building. A celebrated

French teacher thus defines attention: "The Will directing the activity of the Intellect into some particular channel and keeping it there." A weak Will is a sure symptom of a poor memory. The Intellect can not be directed by a weak Will; so the first work to be done in memory development, is to strengthen the Will, and in the first Lesson of this Course some instructions were given in practical methods of increasing the strength of the Will.

Mind-Wandering is the opposite of Attention, and men sometimes speak of mind-wandering as a species of lunacy; so it is evident that the person who cannot fix his attention upon a given proposition or subject and hold it there, is only a little way from the friendly doors of an asylum.

Interest lies at the foundation of Attention. Everybody, the involuntary thinker, the mind-wanderer and the scientific thinker, each finds it easy to fix attention upon anything in which he is deeply interested, and people are usually deeply interested in all matters that concern themselves personally. This is so nearly a universal truism that it may well be said that inability to fix and hold the attention upon a given matter results from a lack of interest in that matter.

All impressions in which men and women are deeply interested, are indelibly fixed in the brain-films, and at any time in life they may be recalled with tolerable alacrity. One often hears people who complain of poor memories tell of some thrilling event in life, even in early life, that made such a deep impression that they recall it in minutest detail, and say, "I never can forget that."

The number of things in which the average person is interested is small, indeed. The selfish person has no care whatever for matters that concern others and not himself. Most people are hobbyists, or faddists, and have but little interest in matters outside of their narrow contracted world, and so their memory bumps are ill-shaped; having just one prominent spur, the rest being depressions, full of dead leaves and passing shadows.

It is only the broad-minded, cosmopolitan man or woman, who can enter fully into the thought-world of humanity and have a heartfelt interest in that which concerns others.

Interest is a Creature of Education, and it must be educated before the memory can be developed; and the question of paramount importance just now is: "How can we become interested in matters that do not concern us personally?" This question takes us back to the first process of memory improvement,

Accurate Observation. There is something in everything to excite sympathy, admiration, curiosity or disgust, and concentrative thinking will bring into prominence that thing. Some minds love detail; others are content with generalities. The detail thinker is the accurate observer, and so it is essential to form the habit of thinking in detail.

Exercises for the Development of the Habit

of Accurate Observation. Take any object, either an object of nature, as a flower or tree, or a machine made by the hand of man, and in the mind take it to pieces, and study its parts. In the case of the machine, study the mechanism of the different parts; note the materials entering into its structure; the kind of wood that would be best suited for the purpose, whether beach or maple, or oak, or ash, or pine, or redwood. Note the kind of metals required in its construction. If iron or steel or copper be used, determine in what part of the earth they were, probably, found. You can then, with profit turn to your Encyclopaedia and learn where the various metals are mined and prepared for use.

One of the best helps in developing the habit of critical observation is the study of manufacturing. Go to the foundry; where they take chunks of pig-iron, and melt them in a great furnace; observe the various processes of converting the crude material into sheets or into rails for car tracks. A little yankeeism is in order; **ask questions** until you are familiar with the whys and the hows on all processes.

The student must have his eyes and ears open continually. Much help may come from sign-reading. As you walk along the street observe the various stores and the order of their location. Read all the signs from First to Seventh street, in any city, and then recall the order of their location.

Go into a library and note the books; first

those on a single shelf; then all in the case; observe the titles and the order in which the books are placed.

I need not give more special exercises in fixing the habit of observing. Every one, anywhere, can find opportunity for practice; but practice, and that continually, is absolutely essential.

Remembering What You Read. The habit of rapid reading, so much in vogue among novel readers, destroys the sensitized films of the brain and leads to quasi idiocy, if not to insanity. Rapid readers are, usually superficial thinkers, and care little for anything but the lightest conventionalities, and seem to pride themselves in their poor memories. What we mean by

Reading is not saying over the words of a book; it is the absorption of the ideas; making that which is offered in the way of intellectual food, a part of one's self. A book is a table spread with things supposed to be good for the stomach of the mind to appropriate, and the same discrimination must be exercised as is in order in selecting food to supply the wants of the physical body. No two persons get the same nourishment from a book; in fact, it is difficult to find two persons who need the same intellectual food, and it takes considerable discretion to know just what is required in a given case.

In reading, as in listening to lectures, we come across ideas that appeal to us, while other ideas that may be equally as important, do not command a moment's thought.

The second reading of a book will usually reveal much appropriate food that did not appear on the first reading. It is fallacy to stuff the mind-stomach with all the intellectual food a book contains at first reading.

Useless Food. Almost every book contains much that the reader does not need, in the form of indigestible ideas, and ideas that have already been appropriated. In reading, that which one well knows need not concern him. With this restriction we are ready to open the book.

The Subject Matter. The first question of the scientific reader is: What is the scope of the work? Every well prepared book has a Table of Contents that gives a general idea of the subject matter. A thorough study of the outline therein given will intensify the interest of the reader, and if he wants to know all there is in the book suitable to his stage of advancement he must approach it with the greatest possible interest.

A Foreword, or Preface, usually precedes the opening chapter. This frequently gives the rate of vibration of the author's thoughts; this should be carefully read, and its relationship to the Table of Contents noted, if for no other purpose than to bring the reader en rapport with the author.

Introductions are sometimes prominent features of books. These are usually written by the author for the same reason that the young artist wrote under his sketch: "This is a horse," for fear no one would be able to tell what it was. A clear cut, concisely written book needs no Introduction. If, however, there is one, and its very presence does not make you feel that the intellectual food the author has placed upon his table is raw or not well cooked, read it, just as you read the Table of Contents. By this time expectancy is on tip-toe, interest has reached its exaltation and you are ready to read the first chapter.

A celebrated French instructor once said: "What is one's object in reading a book? Simply to retain the **Ideas** in it that are **new** and **useful to** him, as well as the **new uses** that are therein set forth of **old and familiar ideas."**

Slow reading with concentrative thinking is just as important in memory building as thorough mastication of food in the upbuilding of the physical body.

Pencil and Paper are indispensible for the critical reader until he has taken the degree M. M.—Master of Memory. Now you are ready to begin; read the first paragraph, and note the new ideas that it contains and the uses to which old ideas are put. Jot down in the most concise manner the information you have received, continue in this way through the chapter, and through the book.

Abstract Making is a science as well as an art which every one can formulate for himself. After a while the reader becomes familiar with his own marks, which may be simply hieroglyphs, and he can reread from his marks every new idea he has found in the book. This process closely followed will enable almost any one to become familiar with all the new ideas he has found in the book.

Book Vibration. Books that have never been read are more difficult to master than books that have been read by a concentrative thinker. If you are a sensitive you have observed this. The eye of the reader magnetizes the page; the thoughts that lie back of the letters of the book are brought out by the critical reader, are taken into his thought amplifier, magnetized and returned in an indelible manner to the page of the book. These returned magnetized thoughts give a marvelous value to the book. A master will give much more for a book that has been read by another master than for one just from the press. In buying books I always try to find those that have been in the libraries of master minds.

Reading Books Unopened. A sensitive seldom finds it necessary to open a book that has been read by a master, in order to become familiar with its ideas. He simply places the book under his head before going to bed and while he sleeps he accumulates the most valuable thoughts that it contains. It is very difficult to get any information in this manner from an unread book.

Accumulation of Knowledge Without Books. This is possible. Whatever others have thought is public property; it is registered upon the ethers, and he who is qualified to do so may read the ideas as readily as he can read from the pages of a printed book. This is the reason that ideas are contagious. A hunded or a thousand men who live in various parts of the earth may simultaneously receive the same idea without reading a book. The true master is not a reader of books, he need not be. The Great Breath is surcharged with all the ideas that have been formulated and when he is familiar with the true Science of the Great Breath he is filled with the wisdom of the ages, is completely saturated with the knowledge of masters living and departed as he sits in his chamber of Silence.

These are the incomparable advantages of Illumination, and every soul who stands upon the cusp of the Fifth-Sixth races is competent to attain unto these great heights.

LESSON III.

COLORS, NATURE'S MEDICINES AND BEAUTIFIERS; WHAT COLORS TO WEAR TO BE ATTRACTIVE AND HEALTHFUL.
LIGHT!

The Manifestor of all Things. The creative God, the Hebrew Elohim, called by the Mystic John in the account of his visions on Patmos, the Seven Spirits of God, were the embodiment of Light, "And God said, Let there be Light, and there was Light."

The Origin of Light need not be considered here; it seems only necessary to state the accepted theory that Light is the result of etheric vibration; that where the ethers are made to vibrate so many times per second the phenomenon called Light is produced, (the required rate of vibration per second is given by scientists at about $35\frac{1}{4}$ trillions, insuring an outward speed of the moving ethers of 186,000 miles per second.)

Light Analysis reveals the fact that there are seven distinct tones, and seven colors in it, and we are informed by the great esoteric masters that each of the creative spirits appropriated one musical tone and one color, as follows: Michael the color red, and the tone C; Raphael the color orange, and the tone D; Gabriel the color yellow, and the tone E; Samael the color green, and the tone F; Uriel the color blue, and the tone G; Zadkiel the color indigo, and the tone A; Cassiel the color violet, and the tone B.

Of course, in the multitudes of combinations of the seven colors we have an indefinite number of shades and tints, and in the combinations of tones we have a great variety of tone waves; but every one can be traced back to its parentage in the Septonate.

It matters not to us just now how colors are produced; it is enough to know that there are seven fairly distinct colors, corresponding to the seven notes of the musical scale.

Color Meanings. There are seven creative principles, as we have already intimated, and each principle has its own specific color and tone. These principles are manifest in the planets of our Solar System and in every thing that has been evolved. He who understands the language of colors can read the history and philosophy of all manifests; even of unmanifest things in vegetable and mineral life.

Powers of Colors. Everything is more or less powerful, and each entity has its own specific character, and the color is the indicator of character.

Color Dictionary .Red is life, vitality; Blood is red, and an ancient physiologist said, "The blood is the life." Red is the color of Force, and taken alone it is blind, ungoverned Force. While it is one of the creative colors it never was capable of acting alone, and the other of the dual primary colors was immediately in evidence.

Blue, the color of Intelligence, flashed into existence, and, like a great mantle covered the power that seemed to be struggling for manifestation. And Blue directed the energies of Red, as Intelligence must ever direct Force.

In celestial chemistry we learn that the pigments of all colors were embraced in Blue and Red, although in the chemistry of our school days we were taught that all other colors could not be made by combining Red and Blue, and our best artists at the present time have not succeeded in doing so. In this operation Transmutation is essential and modern science knows but little about Transmutation.

Yellow is the color of next importance, and it makes but little difference whether we concede that it is the result of the alchemic union of Red and Blue, or is an original pigment, it embraces the characteristics of Force and Intelligence, and the word **Love** quite well defines it.

Old time Theosophists tell us that Yellow means Intelligence and Blue, Love. But one of the most critical seers of the present day says, that Blue means Intellect, Thought, Truth, and that "Yellow is Intuition, Divine Wisdom"—Grumbine, of the order of the White Rose.

In the mystic nomenclature Yellow is accepted as the color of Love.

Among Creative Attributes Red is power; Blue is concentration and cohesion, and Yellow is attractive Discrimination.

Orange results from the union of Red and Yellow; alchemically speaking, of Force and Attractive Discrimination and so it is to a great extent a selfish color. Alchemically it is defined as "Aspiration for the self."

Green results from the union of Yellow and Blue, or of Concentration and Attractive Discrimination, and is a much higher color than Orange, although it has not in it as much of the vital principle. Green is the color of growth and is the symbol of immortality. We speak of it as the color of Aspiration and Hope.

Indigo is but a deeper Blue and means Spiritual Intelligence.

Purple manifests the highest conception of Spiritual unfoldment and is well called **the Truth.**

In the best Dictionaries of colors, Purple is Royalty, Exaltation, Honor, Illumination.

In Secret Doctrine we have the following Table given, which you will observe adopts the mystic color scale, which makes the manifest color of Intelligence Indigo Blue.

Color	State of Matter	Principles
Red.	Ice.	Kama-Rupa, Animal Life.
Orange.	Air.	Prana, or Life Principle.
Yellow.	Water.	Buddhi, Spiritual Soul.
Green.	Air.	Lower Manas, Animal Soul.
Blue.	Steam.	Auric Envelope.
Indigo.	Air.	Spiritual Intelligence, Higher Manas.
Violet.	Ether.	Chhaya, Shadow or Double.

Practical Application of Color. In these studies we are to consider the advantages of color in Personal Attractiveness and in health. Every person is dominated by one of the seven colors, and this domination is so complete that when we know the color that appeals most powerfully to the individual we may have a tolerably clear conception of that person's characteristics. The carnal races and persons, those closest to the physical, admire Red—and these persons are prone to wear red colors—red blankets, red dresses, red hats, red neckties. And they are usually the people of Force, but are not apt to be dominated by Intelligence.

The thoughtful, studious person admires Blue, and if they are spiritually inclined the higher shades of Blue and the Purple appeal to them; and when they can have their own way their garments are decidedly Blue or Purple.

The pure emotional nature, the one who believes that Love is the Universal Savior and whose actions accord with his belief, is ever an admirer of Yellow and this is the predominating color in his attire.

Some masters tell us that the mother Love is the highest manifestation of true Love, and that the color of this Love is a delicate Pink.

I would not for one moment depreciate the exalted nature of mother Love, and still we must confess that it is selfish and clannish. The cord that binds a mother and child is truly sacred, but it is of the flesh, and could not be otherwise than Red in color. It is not the Universal Love of the Christ, which is almost free from the colors of the carnal. Another may have the deepest and most spotless love for her child and not have a shred of love for some body else's child or for universal Life. We must not let sentiment destroy judgment.

Attractiveness Through Color-Blending. As in the indiscriminate mingling of tones we have discordant sounds, so when colors are not blended according to the principles of harmonics, we have a lot of vibrations that are akin to the filing of a saw. When a lady appears with the colors of her garments thrown together, with no reference to the principles of color blending, every sensitive observer cringes as though in a nettle-bed. A few suggestions may be made that will help the lady with non-artistic taste to render herself attractive.

The lady with blue eyes, fair complexion and auburn hair, might wear a light blue dress, trimmed with a darker shade of blue, with white collar, or the entire dress might be trimmed with white. Such a person always looks attractive attired in white. The light blue dress and auburn hair form a harmonic contrast. If, however, the red pigments be prominent in the hair, blue attire is discordant.

The author of Principles of Light and Color says, "Blondes look well in light colored dresses; brunettes in darker ones, while rubicund (reddish) countenances can wear to advantage subdued tints of red."

"If a countenance is too pale, a greenish element will inhance the rosy color by contrast, while a purple tint near the face will bring out the yellow, and give a bilious, sickly appearance.

"If a person's countenance be over-flushed and rosy, a condition which is rarely seen among American ladies, a red ribbon worn near the face will give a paler cast.

"Contrasts of positive colors, such as red and green, blue and orange, yellow and purple, are too glaring to be in good taste, except for military or theatrical costumes. The grays of the same colors are much more tasty and modest.

"Too much of the dark elements in clothing degrades the light into heat, and prevents its finest chemical action on the human system."

Practical Uses of Colors in Health and Disease. Sunlight is the combination of all colors, and is the ne plus ultra of medicines. Houses and clothing are the causes of much of the weakness and misery to which humanity is heir. He who will institute a comparison between the so-called civilized nations and the uncivilized nations will find proofs of this statement. Civilization, disease and drunkenness seem to go hand in hand.

Some years ago Rev. J. G. Wood published a remarkable book on "Uncivilized Races of Men" in which he paid a high tribute to these children of nature. He tells us that they are rarely sick, always strong and are blessed with strong lines of beauty.

Nearly all of the women and many of the men of America, are hot-house plants, who look sickly, smell sickly, act sickly and are sickly. They imagine that houses are built to live in and that clothes are made to wear; so they bundle up with clothes and shut themselves up in houses for fear the sunshine and air might strike their precious forms.

In his balmy days, the great natural hygienist, Dr. Dio Lewis wrote: "Don't you see a good many pale girls in your stores, girls with a bloodless, half baked sort of face, whose whole expression is void of spirit and force? Those girls are in a green state. Look at their lips and cheeks. They are not half ripe. Send them out into the country; let them throw away their parasols and live out in the sunshine three months and I would give more for one of them in any work requiring spirit than for a dozen of those pale things that live in the shade. The only girls with red cheeks and sweet breaths, the only girls who become fully ripe and sweet, are those who baptize themselves in sunshine. For many years I have advised, in the case of a weak, emaciated child, the sun-bath. These little frail half-baked creatures that die of marasmus, would, in hundreds of cases, recover if they could be thoroughly cooked, or baked over in the sun. With magical rapidity I have seen little ghostly, dying things recover by two or three hours daily sleeping or rolling about naked in the sunshine."

Some years ago our rustic poet, Walt Whitman, wrote: "Twelve years ago I came to Camden to die; but every day I went into the country, and naked, bathed in sunshine, lived with the birds and the squirrels, and played in the water with the fishes, I recovered my health."

Beauty is always enhanced by the sunshine. Dr. Babbitt once said: "Sun-exposed bodies gain such activity of the blood forces as to prevent any excessive forming of adipose matter, and hence the ugliness of obesity is avoided. On the other hand the solar rays quicken the nutrient functions so that leanness may be averted or remedied. From these and many other facts that could be given the beautifying effect of sunlight is evident."

If our cadaverous, white faced ladies would throw away their superfluous clothing, their paints, powders, sun-shades and body jackets, fling wide open the doors and windows of their houses (never mind the mosquitoes and flies) and spend every possible moment in God's pure air, and his magnificent sunshine, they would soon begin to be beautiful instead of pretty, the fat and the lean would meet upon a common plane of symmetric figures; sick headache, sick stomach, sick liver and sick lungs would be numbered among the things of the past and a high type of beauty and healthfulness would be the heritage of their children, and they themselves would be loved for what they **are** and not for what they **seemed to be.**

But people are creatures of education, and reforms are of slow growth.

People will not give up their luxurious houses, their superfluous clothing and their sunshades all at once, so we must make a critical study of how we may best help them in their present degenerate stage of civilization.

Chromopathy, or the system of curing diseases by colors, is perhaps the most practical of all systems of healing now knocking for recognition at the doors of science. The atmosphere contains every substance in nature, and the prismatic colors are nature's eliminators. These select and apply to all manifests just what is needed for beauty, health and strength. A table of the healing qualities of colors is here in order.

"**Red** is warming, and especially stimulating to the arterial blood, and is called for in cold, pale or bluish conditions. It is contra-indicated in inflammable and over-excitable conditions.

"**Yellow,** aided by some red (yellow-orange)

is animating to the nerves, being laxitive, diuretic, stimulating to the brain, liver, etc., and especially desirable in paralytic and stupid conditions. It is contra-indicated in delirium, fluidic conditions, etc.

"**Blue, Indigo and Violet,** being cooling and contracting, are nervine, astringent, refrigerant, antiseptic, anti-inflammatory, narcotic and anti-spasmotic. They are contra-indicated in cold bluish and chronic conditions, unless considerable excitibility is present.

"**Green** is mainly cooling and much like the blue as strained through ordinary green glass, though the yellow part of green gives some nerve stimulus.

"**Purple** combines the blood warming red and the cooling antiseptic blue, and is excellent for lungs, stomach, kidneys and other parts where animation without irritation is needed.

"**Orange** arouses the nerves and to some extent, the blood."

How to Apply the Colors. Many ways have been suggested, but one of the best methods is by the clothing that is worn, and the colorings of the rooms in which one lives.

If one is suffering from inertia, lack of vitality, collapse, because of blood poverty, paralysis, etc., the color red is indicated. All other positive colors should be removed from the living room and the clothing; red should predominate in every way; the under clothing sould be red. Most cases of consumption where the blood is greatly impoverished, this red medication will prove curative.

In all inflammatory conditions, fevers, inflammatory rheumatism, the red treatment is contra-indicated. All red should be eliminated from the ceilings and furnishings of living rooms and from garments worn. Red flowers increase the suffering of persons afflicted with inflammatory conditions.

If the system be sluggish and all parts of the body are clogged; in all conditions where cathartics are seemingly called for, attention should be directed at once to the color **Yellow;** it is of more value than aloes, podophyllum, Syrup of Figs, Carter's Little Liver pills and salts, combined. Yellow furnishings of living apartments, yellow clothing, and foods that contain yellow pigment will speedily restore harmonious conditions and insure health. Yellow is contra-indicated in all fluidic conditions.

Blue is the fever remedy par **excellence.** This color and Indigo have such power over inflammatory conditions that when a patient is entirely dominated by these colors other remedies are seldom called for. These are also narcotic, anti-spasmodic and nerve sedatives, and since most American women are troubled with insomnia, some sort of spasms or what they call nervousness, these should constitute the prominent colors in all dress goods and head wear.

Frequently blue might not be especially becoming to a certain style of beauty; still for health's sake one may be forced to outrage aesthetic taste for a little time.

Green has many of the effects of the blue, and in some conditions may be substituted with profit.

Colored Glass occupies a prominent place in the armamentarium of a Chromopathic healer; but as the directions given in the matter of wearing apparel cover the entire philosophy we need not now consider the methods of using glass.

Colors are Powerful Eliminators; and with the aid of proper appliances will gather from the atmosphere any substance ever required in healing.

LESSON IV.

THE SECRET OF POPULARITY AND LEADERSHIP; SHORT CUTS TO PERSONAL MAGNETISM

The well-poised, symmetrically developed person is always popular. Cranks are just on one side of the grindstone, and though they may everlastingly keep things turning and stirred up, and may be popular with many people for a little time, and a few people for a long time, they never attain to anything like universal popularity.

When men or women attain to leadership and popularity, their characters demand critical study; there is something in them more than the ordinary, and whoever can find the key to their successes may be benefitted.

What is the Secret of Popularity? It is not education; for among those not educated we find as many popular people, as we do among those who are educated. It is not piety; for the rough man of the world is just as apt to be the idol of the populace as the most devout religionist. It is not aesthetic culture; for the woman with only a moity of refinement may outstrip her cultured sister in popularity.

In searching for the secret of leadership we find an undefinable something in the personality of the individual. When you stand in the presence of a people's favorite you intuitively feel a force that seems to draw you almost irresistibly to his person. That something is the secret of popularity, and that something is an inherent quality of all people, and may be developed so that popularity will be universal.

Native Popularity is no uncommon thing. Some babies are everybodies favorites before they are a week old. And this is not because they are so entrancingly beautiful, or so markedly intelligent; but some how they differ from other babies and every passer-by has an overpowering desire to snatch them up and kiss them.

And it isn't a question of heredity; for coarse, crude parents may bring into the world a little one who is the center of attraction from the moment of birth. These children may with propriety be called

Natural Favorites. But Theosophists tell us that there are no such personalities; that the All-Loving-Father is no respecter of persons; that he pours out his choicest blessings upon all alike, and all just persons cannot help saying, Selah; for God would not be just if he did otherwise.

But that seeming favorites do appear every one knows, and we appeal to a Mahatma for a solution of the mystery, and the Mahatma answers:

"This life is but a little span of the great life of man. The true home of every individuality is in the realm of the Invisebles, and all are born into this earth-life very frequently for experiences—for the purpose of unfolding every attribute of the Infinite One, which enters into the composition of every Ego. In the course of Ages one may have visited these earth planes of experience many times and gradual unfoldment is marked. That brilliant child that men call a favorite has spent many years amid the buffeting of earth scenes in order to attain unto its present place of popularity and leadership. No one knows what it has had to suffer and endure in other lives. The child that is not now a favorite will, some day, be born a favorite, for the blessings that are in store for one are in store for all."

Prodigies are Found. And this philosophy accounts for the many that come to earth—our wonderful child musicians, mathematicians, artists and orators.

But the popular baby may not be in any sense of the term a prodigy; what, then is the secret of its popularity? Look at it well, and you will note strange lines radiating from its person; it is a living mass of attractive magnetism; its magnetic aura reaches out to great distances. This magnetic soul is not the offspring of a few months. By determined efforts in other lives it has developed this magnetic power; but you may be sure that it has gained all that it has by heroic effort, and every one will do the same; but in this marvelous age of spirit one may crowd his development so that in this life he may enjoy much of the rich fruit of his labors. And this brings us to the consideration of

Acquired Popularity. All leaders of the people, all favorites, are magnetic personalities, and most magnetic personalities are, in a great measure favorites, and so a study of personal magnetism and how it may be obtained along the lines of least resistance is the question of the hour.

In the mystic analysis of man and his bodies, for he has more than one, we have the beginning of the true explanatory philosophy. For our present purpose we may look at man as a pentad, as possessing five bodies. Omitting all Orientalisms and Hindu nomenclature we find that the three primary bodies correspond with the three primary tones of the musical scale C, E and G, and the three primary colors, red, yellow and blue. Paul recognized the bodily trinity when he said: "I pray God that your whole being, body, soul and Spirit, be preserved blameless in the presence of the Christ."

The Human Trinity and its correspondences may be thus stated: The physical body is the red of color and the C of music; the soul is the yellow of color and the E of music, the Spirit is the blue of color and the G of music. As in music C is the key-note and G is the dominant note, so in the human scale the physical body is the key-note, because it manifests the rest of the scale and the Spirit is the dominant note.

Connecting Bodies. Between the physical body and the soul we find a correlative body as a connecting link, and this uniting body is to all appearances exactly like the physical in form. This body is sometimes called the Etheric body; sometimes Desire body, for in it lie all the strains of desire that must be worked out before one can complete his circles of carnal births. It corresponds to the orange in color and D in music. The elements of selfishness are found in this connecting body, and we learned in our study of color meanings in our last lesson that orange means: "Aspirations for self."

Between the soul and the Spirit we find another connecting body that is in form exactly like the physical or the soul, but in character it is higher than either, because it is, largely free from carnal desires. We call this connecting body the magnetic and corresponds to the green of the color scale and the F of music. It is this body that carries in to both soul and the physical, the true genius of the higher Ego, the Spirit.

And thus we have before us the man as a pentad—five bodied. Thus considered he is the vital star, the star of promise, the star of Bethlehem, the star of hope.

The Prime Characteristics of these five bodies may be expressed thus:

1. The physical body exhibits the carnal nature.
2. The etheric body the emotional nature.
3. The soul body the aspirational nature.
4. The magnetic body the dynamic nature.
5. The Spirit body the Spiritual or God nature.

In the magnetic body we find the potentialities, the force, of the entire being, and when this is properly unfolded the individual upon the higher planes, and the person upon the physical plane, becomes a power that is simply irresistable, and this is what we mean by

Personal Magnetism; and this is that indefinable something that elevates failure into success, and is the true key of popularity and leadership. How, then, may we develop this magnetic, this fourth body of the human pentad? How may we become magnetic and be able to exclaim with the resurrected Nazarine, "All power is given unto me in heaven and in earth."

Foods. These are required in order to insure the growth of anything; but no two kinds of entities require exactly the same kinds of food.

These five bodies of man must be fed, and the great oversoul, who formed the bodies, created and scattered through all worlds with a lavish hand the food that each requires.

Source of Food. The so-called atmospheric envelopment of our earth is a wonderful compound; but mark, it is not a chemical compound in which the ingredients are indissolubly bound together as we find them in the ates and ides of the chemical laboratory. It is a mechanical mixture, in which the almost endless kinds of life foods are mixed, as we might mix beans and corn and barley and wheat. In this atmosphere we find five principal kinds of food designed for the five lower bodies of man.

Now, each body is a learned discriminator and selects from these boundless granaries of nature the specific food that will nourish it.

How to Appropriate this Food that the world knows not of, the bread from heaven, is the question of paramount importance. These ethers that contain the foods for all life is the Great Breath, which is a matter of theoretic analysis. Ancient mystics, even more modern Orientalists have done much in the way of analyzing the Great Breath, but their elaborateness in analysis has carried the subject entirely through the domain of clearness into a dense murkiness, and it takes a pretty good reasoner to understand what the Hindus mean in their analysis. In the clearer language of Western thought we may present the matter thus:

There are five kinds of food in the air we

breathe, and each kind has a special affinity and is drawn toward one or the other of the five bodies of man. Because of man's descent into matter the receptive avenues for the prehension of these foods have been charged with numberless resistance molecules, and they are not readily appropriated. The carnal emotions, such as fear, anger, hate, jealousy, envy, revenge, offer strong resistance, and nearly cut off the food supply from the higher bodies.

This resistance must be overcome, these foreign substances that the carnal self has injected into the great arteries of life, must be dissolved, and, hence, the necessity of **purifying the heart by faith,** as the early Christine teachers taught. That all these food-ethers may have free access to the bodies they are designed to nourish, the aspirant must be pure in thought and word and deed.

Thought is the thing in the universe that can "fix the volatile and volatilize the fixed," and, hence, Thought potentized by Will, is the great Scavenger of life's highways.

Men once knew how to breathe and thus to fully appreciate the Great Breath; but in their mad rush for wealth and carnal pleasures they have forgotten their muck rakes, their shovels and their brooms and all the avenues of breath have become so clogged with alchemic filth that even the lungs have shriveled up so that their capacity is only a fractional part of what it should be. Not more than one-fourth of the lung cells are engaged in the process of ordinary breathing; in the majority of people the upper lobes of the lungs, yes, and the lower lobes, too, are absolutely inert for lack of use. Stagnation is on and sooner or later inflammation will set in, resolution will follow and the undertaker and grave digger will shortly close the scene.

Scientists everywhere are busy with the solution of the Consumption problem, and medical experts are delving down into the depths of all manner of filth, hunting for a serum or lymph that will cure this dread disease. Oh, the foolishness of modern Science! It is just tampering with the topmost boughs of the great Upas tree while the roots are getting stronger every day.

An ounce of prevention is worth a car-load of cure, and the critical masters of all times tell us no organ is ever diseased amid the environments of judicious activity. No natural breather ever had the Consumption; and so the great work of the humanitarian is to teach men and women **how to breathe.**

The Organs of Breathing are not confined to a few inches in the chest embracing the lungs, only. The natural breather breaths with every inch of his body, provided the skin is kept clean. The skin of an ordinary person contains over seven million pores, and every one of them is a miniature lung, and is constantly employed in the processes of true breathing.

There are two processes of life—**Expansion** and **Contraction,** and the average person is an adept in the use of the latter; he knows how to contract, but he hasn't the slightest conception of expansion. In even ordinary breathing, if it is perfomed with half the zeal that one exhibits in other matters its force will increase the size and intensify the power of any part of the body on which thought is concentrated. Remember that thought is the cleanser and the creator, and he who will concentrate that thought upon any shrunken or diseased tissue as he inhales and exhales to the limit of his capacity, will bring that part into a condition of wholeness.

Personal Magnetism, which insures popularity and just recognition among the masses, depends mainly upon this first one of the divisions of the Great Breath, which with propriety might be called: **The Breath of Animal Life**—the breath that gathers from the atmosphere the true food to sustain and develop the physical body.

The true Science of the Great Breath must be understood before one can know the value of breathing. The color of the Breath of Animal Life is red, and its musical tone is C.

The Breath of Aspiration is recognized as the Second of the vital breaths. The ethers of Aspiration for self are everywhere abundant, and these constitute the food of the Desire body, that etheric connection between physical body and soul. Its color is Orange and its musical note is D. We have already learned that Orange is the color of Aspiration for self.

The most prominent characteristic of this etheric body is Ambition, which in its place must not be handicapped, or there can be no development. The person who lacks Ambition is a sluggard, is never popular, cannot be a leader, and is too indolent to be led. The man without Ambition knows nothing about the power of this Orange breath. If he could only get one taste of this magnificent food he would rise as if by enchantment from his bed of carnal security and littleness into a new world.

The Breath of the Heart. By this name we know the Third of the Vital Breaths. It is the breath that brings in the food to feed the soul. It enhances the powers of the deeper emotional nature, and fills the entire being with that indefinable something that distinguishes the true lover from the Platonist. He who understands and makes daily use of the Breath of the Heart is universally loved. Lovesick swains pay vast sums of money for fake nostrums to compel the prime object of their heart's desire to love them. The world is full of love powders, and honeydrops and passion charged candies that foolish lassies take from the hands of designing culprits, which temporarily set their poor brains on fire, and they imagine they love, only to find out that their forced love is a mushroom that will wither when the illusion is dispelled and the true sun shines forth. Then love is turned into disgust.

Men and women, if you want to be loved,

make yourself lovable. Learn how to breathe the Breath of the Heart, and you need never meddle with the heart-strings of another in order to provoke love.

The color of the Breath of the Heart is Yellow, and its musical note E.

The Magnetic Breath is the appropriate name of that truly higher breath that brings in the sustenance of the magnetic body which unites the soul and the spirit. This breath is one of superior power, and when a person knows how to appropriate the three inferior breaths he may use the magnetic breath in such a way as to make him a Lord among Lords, and bring him to the highest plane of leadership. Men sometimes speak of this as the Breath of Hope; but I think that it carries one to the realms far beyond hope; it is the Breath of Realization. Its color is Green, and its musical note is F.

The Breath of the Spirit, sometimes called the Holy Breath, or the Holy Spirit, is the ne plus ultra of the breaths that men can appropriate while they tabernacle here in the flesh. Once the Christian Apostles breathed upon certain far-advance disciples and said: "Receive ye the Holy Breath." This breath of true Inspiration brings one into the higher ethers where the River of Life flows unsullied from the Divine Throne, where the Trees of Immortal Life grow in their beauty; where the Fountain of Wisdom flows on forever and where the Sun of Righteousness floods all the plains with the light of health and deathlessness. The color of the Spirit Breath is Blue and its musical tone is G, the dominant tone in the Divine Scale.

This is the breath referred to by the great Nazarine when he said: "I have yet many things to say unto you, but you cannot bear them now; but when she, the Spirit of Truth (the Holy Breath) is come, she will guide you into all truth."

Glorious Breath! and the encouraging part of all is that every human being may become the abiding place of this Divine Breath.

This completes my lesson. The master of the Science of the Great Breath is the master of time and eternity. Men and women, the gates are wide ajar; arise and enter into the joys of your Lord.

LESSSON V.

UNFOLDING THE POWERS OF THE SOUL

The spirit of man is the true Ego; the soul is the shadow of the Ego; the physical body is the shadow of the shadow.

In a sense both soul and body are illusions, for both will pass away; the spirit is the only real; for it only abideth forever. In another sense, both the soul and the physical body are realities, for in both these are essences that are imperishable. The Christian Apostle Paul referred to this enduring quality of all parts of the triune man when he wrote: "I pray God that your whole being, Spirit, soul and body, be preserved blameless in the presence of the Christ."

In this sense Mystics believe in physical immortality, the age enduring character of the body.

The Physical Body is an entity capable of development, whether we view it as an illusion or a real, and the higher it is developed, the more tangible and powerful will the immortal essence of it become. It has ever been considered by great masters as a Temple, an abiding place for the Great Breath and, therefore, should be kept pure, and developed in all its parts.

The Soul Body is capable of being unfolded, not developed. It is thought that men usually understand what we mean by the Soul Body much better when we speak of it as the Mind Body, since it embraces all the faculties, functions and attributes of mind. Our intellectual powers and emotions, our loves and jealousies, our hates and our desires have their origin in the soul. On this carnal plane they are manifest through the physical body, and the character of the machinery being more or less gross, the emotions are liable to partake of the nature of animalism.

The Spirit is the true Ego, the germ formulated in the Divine Breath; really the seed from which perfected manhood must spring. The life of man on all planes of existence is evolved as a helper in the unfoldment of this true Ego.

The old catechism asks: "What is the chief end of man?" The answer is, "To glorify God and enjoy him forever."

The new catechism asks: "What is the chief end of man?" The answer is, "To unfold the Spirit germ, and bring the Ego into the perfection of its kind."

So while we develop the body and unfold

the soul, we are perfecting the true man. Nothing is ever lost that is done to enhance the beauty of form or feature; for all such efforts add to the perfection of the spirit. True beauty is deeper than the skin and abides forever.

The unfoldment of our moral, intellectual and spiritual powers is never lost; but is so much gain in the chief work of man—the perfection of the spirit. We sometimes think that when a young man or woman has spent the springtime of life in study and research, in attaining intellectual power and aesthetic taste, and is then called away by death, that all is lost, **I tell thee, nay**; not one effort in the way of true development or unfoldment is ever wasted. The accountant of Eternity puts every effort to the credit of the Ego, and when the final balance sheet is struck, every effort will appear on the credit side of the ledger, and it matters not whether these efforts have, in the eyes of men, resulted in success or failure. It is the **effort** that counts and not what men call results.

It is, indeed, hard for men to judge accurately of successes in life. One may put forth ordinary efforts and achieve great success, and another may put forth efforts equally as strong and fail in every particular, and the short-visioned human critic elevates one to the throne of honor, and relegates the other to the depths of degradation. But **God** knows and judges in justice. There are drunkards in the ditch, so-called criminals in the penitentiary, and courtisans in brothels, who are immeasurably higher in the sight of God than the juries and judges and the white-washed men and women who have still about them the gauzy cloak of respectability, and were the instruments by which these so-called failures in life have been consigned to their filthy prisons. Oh, the sham and shoddy of modern respectability. If half of the secret corruption of so-called respectable society could be revealed the hideous glare of the red light district would pale into utter insignificance.

Unfolding the Powers of the Soul; this is the theme of this study. We have already noted that the powers of the soul are the powers of the mind, so our work comprises the unfoldment of intellectual, moral and spiritual strength, and aesthetic taste.

The Soul is a body like the physical; or perhaps it would be better to say that the physical is built according to the pattern of the soul. The soul senses correspond exactly with the physical; the soul sees, hears, smells, tastes, feels and telepaths. Through these senses it obtains its information, and through these senses we must approach it in our work of unfoldment.

The Gateway of the Soul, or the door between the soul and the physical body, must be opened up before we can intelligently enter the work of soul unfoldment. Without opening up this door the work may go on; but when one is not conscious of what he is doing it is indeed hard to retain an interest in his work, and, he is liable to give it all up in despair. I may tell you that, separate from the body your soul makes journeys in the Astral, night after night, but if you cannot bring back to the plane of objective consciousness a knowledge of such soul flights the whole affair is to you a myth, and you can scarcely be blamed when you say that I just imagine such things; that there are no soul activities apart from the body.

So our first step in soul-power unfoldment is to give to you the key that will unlock the

Door of the Veil. We speak of **the** door, as though there were but one; and still we may recognize things by the help of either of the senses. We may see, hear, feel, smell or taste the living ethers of astral things, and thus find an inspiration to faith.

Unfolding the Senses. Physical beings quite readily sense perfumes that come from the plane of the soul; and so the door of the veil may most easily be opened by the sense of smell. It is no uncommon thing for most persons to recognize odors that are not products of any earthly object. As men have passed over the burning sands of the desert, many miles from any sort of vegetation they have been regaled with the perfumes of roses, lilies, violets, pinks and other flowers. They have caught the peculiar odor of the pine, the eucalyptus, the acasia, the magnolia and the cinamon tree, though no such trees were within a hundred miles of them on the earth plane.

And they have asked, from whence? and physical science answers; no such perfumes were there; it is all the result of imagination; but the Occult master says, those delicious perfumes were there; they came from the blooming flowers in the gardens of the soul world, and from the great trees that grow on the banks of the River of Life.

But these perfumes come to us at any place, and we may unfold the sense of smell, so that we may at will open up this gate of astral odors.

Opening the Gate of Soul Perfumes. Go into a room entirely free from substances that could possibly produce an odor or perfume. Take a comfortable position and enter the Silence, according to the rules we have often given. Take one full breath, followed by a searching, purifying, or cleansing breath according to the formula given. Put in abeyance all of the senses except that of smell, and then in mind bring before you a particular flower, or a substance that you know will emit a particular odor; rivet your attention upon this imaginary object for some minutes, and then imagine that you can smell that particular odor, and in a large per cent of such efforts you will be rewarded with a true materialization of the desired odor. But don't be discouraged; if you do not succeed at first, make other efforts and success will come.

Opening the Gate of Soul Flavors. Next to the sense of smell, that of taste is the most sensitive. Smell and taste are so very closely related that when the nostrils are closed taste is not perfect.

The method given for unfolding the sense of smell may be used in opening the Gate of Soul Flavors, except, that all the sense avenues except that of taste are closed, and then by force of Will we bring the Astral flavors to the taste bulbs.

Opening the Gate of Vision. It is thought that men and women find more pleasure in the sense of vision than in all the others. People are everywhere intensely anxious to see that which is beyond the veil, and while it is much more difficult to see Astral scenes than to smell Astral perfumes or taste Astral flavors, people have put forth such great efforts to see that clairvoyance is a nearer universal accomplishment than either of the others. However, many of the methods that have been employed to "develop" clairvoyant vision have been exceedingly harmful to the person, in many ways, often driving the experimenter into insanity.

Safe Methods. There are many of them; and these we will give without describing those that are unsafe. The first question that may with propriety be asked is, why can some people see clairvoyantly while others can not? A little study of Alchemic physiology will discover the answer. The connection between the optic ganglia of the physical eye and that of the soul eye has been charged with opaque molecules, and these are, mostly accumulations deposited by carnal desires and unholy emotions. Sometimes, however, they are inherited obstructions, and sometimes physiologic deposits. But they are so nearly all the results of the carnal desires of this or preceding lives that an Occult poet was once moved to write:

"No curtain hides from view the sphere elysian
  Save these poor shells of half-transparent dust;
And all that hides the spiritual vision
  Is pride, and hate and lust."

This poetic sentiment is not absolutely correct, for if it were none but the pure in heart could see clairvoyantly, while we all know that often villians and licentious people see as clearly on the lower planes of the Astral as do true saints. In the light of spiritual clairvoyance, however, the sentiment of the poet is correct, for none but the pure in heart can see God or the sacred scenes of the spiritual planes.

Dependent and Independent Vision are possible. By Dependent Vision we mean lucidity produced by the help of other influences; by Independent Vision we mean a lucidity attained by personal efforts alone.

Drugs and hypnotism are the two most powerful helps in the production of Dependent Clairvoyance; but as both are dangerous and transitory in effect they ought never to be resorted to. The only clairvoyance that is worthy of the name is that which may be acquired without extraneous helps, and this only may be considered in this study of Unfolding the Powers of the Soul.

The Method. Prepare as in opening up the gates of perfume and taste. Go into the Silence and take the full Breath of Life, which must be followed by the Master's Psychic Breath, so well described in other courses of Instruction. Then make of thought a "sharp two-edged sword which is able to pierce to the dividing asunder of soul and spirit, and of the joints and marrow," as Paul intimated in Heb. 4:12. Now close the eyes tightly and look intently, and you will see thousands of points of light; select a single point, and bring into service your sharp sword of thought, and extend the selected point of light in every direction. These points are but small openings in the veil that separates the photospheric light from the atmospheric light, the physical from the astral.

Most people are surprised at the results of the first sitting. The veil seems to open as if by enchantment, and the whole realm of the soul spreads out like a panorama of beauty.

Opening the Gate of Hearing. Our atmosphere is filled with sounds too refined for human ears to hear. The auditory apparatus of the human head is only able to bring the ethers up to a given rate of vibration, which enables one to hear certain crude sounds, while the sweeter melodies of nature are not heard. These sweeter sounds are astral, where the "music of the spheres" is produced. Whatever increases the rate of vibration of the sonoriferous ethers extends the range of hearing; so if we can find a means of doing this we have found the key to the Gate of Soul Hearing, or clairaudience.

We know that naught increases the rate of etheric vibration but Thought and he who can potentize his Thought and bring it to bear in the proper manner, has accomplished his purpose.

Method. Find the Silence and take the Psychic Breath as directed in Opening the Gate of Vision. Shut off all the sense avenues except that of hearing; first listen for the tinkling of a bell in the dreamy distance. Hold this thought until the bell really rings; then listen for other sounds, never yielding nor giving up the thought until you have heard the sound you have idealized.

In the Book of the Golden Precepts the master gives the steps in hearing in these words:

"Before thou settest thy foot upon the ladder's upper rung, the ladder of mystic sounds, thou must hear the voice of thy inner God in seven manners:

"**The First** is like the nightingale's sweet voice, chanting a song of parting to its mate.

"**The Second** comes as the sound of a silver cymbal of the Dhyanis, awakening the twinkling stars.

"**The Third** is like the plaint melody of the ocean-sprite imprisoned in a shell.

The Fourth is a sweet melody, like the

chant of vina (an ancient musical instrument like the lute).

"**The Fifth** is like the shrill sound of a bamboo flute, which suddenly changes into the **Sixth,** which resembles the trumpet blast.

"**The Seventh** is like a roll of distant thunder, which swallows all the other sounds; then sound dies away and is heard no more forever."

Mark, this realm of the **Soundless Sound** is the plane of the spirit, where the help of senses is never required. Here are the ethers of universal knowledge where men know without hearing, seeing, feeling, smelling or tasting.

Opening the Gate of Touch. This sense enables one to gain information by coming in contact with objects. The sentient nerves extend to all parts of the body, and every one is provided with a receiving apparatus, so exceedingly sensitive that it is able to recognize the slightest movements of the ethers. In highly organized persons the breath of a passing angel or of certain of the astral entities is perceptibly felt. This delicate sense enables one to gather a wonderful fund of information, that is often ascribed to the higher sense of Intuition.

When this sense is properly unfolded, a vast range of psychic knowledge may be brought under the dominion of the individual.

Method of Unfoldment. The first steps in the unfoldment of each sense is the same. When the Silence has been reached, concentrate attention upon some particular part of the body (the forehead, cheek, lips and back of hand are super-sensitive), and then **Will** that this part shall become more sensitive, continue this Willing for a few moments and then relax every muscle of the body; just wait in an expectant attitude, and note impressions.

A passing astral form may fan the part, or it may breathe upon the part, and you feel as though you were sitting in a draught of air. When you have succeeded in **feeling** impressions on the selected part, then choose another part. If you have succeeded in putting all the other senses in abeyance for the time being, you are pretty sure to receive impressions at the very first sitting.

These impressions may not always be pleasurable, for we must know that the astral world is full of entities of all kinds, good, bad and indifferent, and until one has become a master of Sensation, and can put his aura in a condition of safety, so that evil influences cannot penetrate it, he is liable to be annoyed with ungodly raps and uncanny brushings by unpleasant forces.

Importance of the Sense of Touch. It is, indeed, hard to overestimate it. It is so near akin to the higher sense of Intuition that when it is well unfolded one seems to know almost all things without learning them in the usual way, and this is an accomplishment that is within the reach of everybody.

The Higher Work of Unfolding Soul Powers will be considered in our next lesson. In this lesson we have simply revealed the five keys to enable one to open up the gates of the soul. Through these doors every one should be able to come into the presence of his own soul, where he may learn of its qualities and attributes, and be prepared to do much in the way of unfolding them.

He who can recognize his own soul in its own domain has the key to all power in heaven and on earth.

LESSON VI.

THE HELPFULNESS OF UNSEEN FORCES IN INDIVIDUAL UNFOLDMENT; MAGICAL OPERATIONS

Magic. Men have talked about it in all ages of the world. It has been praised as the ne plus ultra of Sciences; it has been cursed as the philosophy of demons. Nothing has received more attention at the hands of the masses, yet nothing has been so completely misunderstood.

The Magician is the Master of Magic, and in one age he is branded as a vile wizard; in another age he is worshipped as a God. In centuries recently gone he has been esteemed a criminal, a culprit, and has been persecuted because of his supposed intimacy with devils, and "wicked spirit in the regions of the air." In some countries even to this day, every misfortune that befalls men or their possessions; every evil that comes upon village, city, state or nation, is charged to the account of these so-called nefarious demons scornfully called magicians.

The best men of earth have been ostracized from society, spurned, yea, put to death because they possessed powers beyond the ordinary herd of humanity; because they were magicians.

The Magician is the True Initiate. A hundred years ago the great mystic Elephas Levi referred to Initiation and the common fate of Magical Initiates in language worth preserving. He wrote: "Initiation is the preservative against the false lights of mysticism; it equips reason with its relative value, and propositional infallibility connecting it with supreme reason by the chain of analogies. Hence, the initiate knows no doubtful hopes, no absurd fears, because he has no irrational beliefs; he is acquainted with the extent of his powers, and he can dare without danger For him, therefore, to dare is to be able. Here is a new interpretation of his attributes; his lamp represents learning, the mantle which enwraps him, his discretion, and his staff is the emblem of his strength and daring. **'He knows, he dares and is silent.'** He knows the secret of the future, he dares in the present and he is silent on the past. He knows the principles of all symbolism and all religions; he dares to practice or abstain from them without hypocrisy and without impiety; and he is silent upon the one dogma of supreme initiation. He knows the existence and nature of the great magical agent; he dares perform the acts and give utterance to the words which make it subject to human will, and is silent upon the mysteries of the great arcanum.

"So you will find him often melancholy, never dejected or despairing; often poor, never abject or miserable; persecuted often, never disheartened or conquered. He remembers the bereavement and murder of Orpeus, the exile and lonely death of Moses, the martyrdom of the prophets, the tortures of Apollonius, the cross of Jesus. He knows the desolation in which Agrippa died, whose memory is even now slandered; he knows what labors overcame the great Paracelsus, and all that Raymond Lully was condemned to undergo that he might finish by a violent death. He remembers Swedenborg simulating madness and even losing reason in order to excuse his science; St. Martins and his hidden life; Cagliostro, who perished forsaken in the cell of the inquisition; Cazotte, who ascended the scaffold.

"Inheritor of so many victims he does not dare the less, but he understands better the necessity for silence. Let us follow his example; let us learn diligently; when we know, let us have courage, and let us be silent."

Thus hath deposed one of the greatest lights of modern times, who well knew of the powers and the dangers of a true magician, and we must enter the domain of magic with a knowledge of the fact that while we may be able to comprehend something of the true magical agent we will incur the enmity of the ignoramuses who know nothing unless they can taste it in their tea and coffee or smell it in their tobacco. It is the very little man who believes that there is nothing that he cannot see, and that the sum of all knowledge rises and sets in his diminutive head.

Magical Operations all belong to the realm of unseen forces, and he who can make use of these forces is in very truth a magician, and in our study of "The helpfulness of Unseen Forces in Individual Unfoldment" we must enter the domain of magic.

Definition. A celebrated occult writer has given this definition of magic: "The highest science, or wisdom based upon knowledge and practical experience."

Another definition of more practical value is given by the same author in this words: "The art of magic is the art of employing invisible or so-called spiritual agencies to obtain certain visible results." God the supreme magician, makes all things according to the eternal law of magic.

Paul wrote: "Through faith we understand that the worlds were framed by the word of God, so that things which are seen were not made of things that do appear." Heb. 11:3.

Under the Law of Magic creation proceeds; all things grow; psychical and spiritual life unfold. The so-called natural man knows little of causes, and, bat-like, blinded by the brilliant photospheric light, he declares against cause and says: "There is no God; magic is a myth."

Hartman said, "A seed does not become a tree, nor a child a man, by having substance added to its organism by some outside workman, or like a house that is built by putting stones on the top of each other; but living things grow by the action of an internal force, acting from a center within the form. To this center flow the influences coming from the universal store house of matter and motion, and from there they radiate again towards the periphery, and perform that labor which builds up the living organism."

That Unseen Force. We often speak of forces, as though there were many, when in fact there is but One, and that is one of the Attributes of Universal Spirit. There are, however, many forms of power that spring from the one force. There are seven such forms of which we might speak; but the three primary powers well cover all the work of the present study. These are **Electricity, Magnetism, Azothel.** These are all free agents, filling all space.

Electricity has been studied by our scientists; they have gathered it from the atmosphere in immense quantities; they have harnessed it, made it carry our messages, light our streets and homes and turn our machinery. Men would scarcely know how to exist today if the current knowledge of Electricity should be at once lost. But we have learned only a little about this wonderful agent. Electrical science is yet in its infancy. In fifty years from now the knowledge that men will possess of it will enable it to be used in every department of business activity, and the end will not be yet.

Magnetism is a much finer form of power, of which men know but little. We know that it is the power that swings men and women upon the popular tide, that makes the orator irresistable, that inspires leadership, that makes the healing of disease a possibility. But it is too fine to be readily seized by the best machines that man has yet invented; so he has not been able to harness it up as he has Electricity. In this field we have wonderful opportunities for experimentation and invention.

Azothel is the name given to a power immeasurably finer and more powerful than either Electricity or Magnetism. In Bulwer-Lytton's wonderful book, The Coming Race, this power is called

Vril, and the prophetic author was able to look along the vista of coming years and see this marvelous force harnessed up as we now harness Electricity, only by means of machinery simple in form and inexpensive. This power is now unconsciously used by Tesla, Marconi, Edison and others in their wireless telegraphy, telephone and other modern inventions in transmission of scenes, pictures, thoughts and dynamic energy.

This universal Azothel is the mighty agent that will revolutionize all the affairs of men, and many who hear me now will live to see the display of its marvels.

The Operators. Power itself is not intelligent; it is simply dynamic energy, and must be operated by intelligence. These three powers of which we are now speaking, have their intelligent operators everywhere in space. We speak of them as living Spirits—the Spirits of Electricity, of Magnetism, of Azothel; and this is well. It is only through these legions of little operators that men can come in touch with these powers. Physical science, that knows but little of the resources of thought, has sought to capture these Spirits by mechanical appliances, and harness them up with physical straps and iron gearings, and it has succeeded admirably; but the coming race will repudiate all such appliances, and because of the superior spiritual intelligence of the people they will call directly to their aid these unseen powers, and they will be able to speak and it will be done, to command and it will stand fast.

Some of Nature's Manifest Operators may be mentioned. Birds and fishes have always made use of these powers without any appliances, except their own bodies. Birds will dart through the air and fish through the water great distances without moving a feather or a fin, and scientists have been content to say, "They do so according to natural law; but they have no means of explaining that natural law. The next generation of scientists, who will know more of the laws of **Celestial Dynamics,** will tell us **how** birds fly and fishes swim.

Human Dynamics. These must be considered in answering the question of the hour; How to use unseen powers in individual unfoldment.

The human body is a universal dynamo. It is organized in such a way that it may appropriate every power in the universe. It is a natural steam engine forever running, and the steam is generated by the fires of life. Every human being is a fire-eater; he breathes in the oxygen, which in the system is burned up to produce the heat of the body, and keep the dynamo running, so that it can make use of the Electric, Magnetic and Azothic ethers, or powers.

The Great Breath contains every power; Will is the discriminator and when man puts himself in a receptive attitude, he can command and the desired power will come, which will be appropriated by his powerful dynamo, and the work is done.

Methods. How to attract the specific powers. This is the culminating problem of our present study. Bearing in mind these postulates:

1. All the powers exist free and untrammeled in the air we breathe.

2. All the powers are subject to the will of man.

We are ready to proceed with the magical operation.

Cleansing the Dynamo. No machine can do good work until it is thoroughly cleansed, and the human dynamo is no exception. Oxygen and its soul mate are the scavengers of body and soul, and when these are properly inhaled and exhaled, all worn out substances and resistance molecules will be removed, and the dynamo will be in condition to do good work.

How. That which we concentrate our thought upon in a commanding manner, while we breathe, will materialize. We then place ourselves in a comfortable position, and with the thought of **cleansing** uppermost in mind, we inhale, through the nostrils, of course, filling the lungs, yea, every part of the body, with pure air; then, with the thought of cleansing still in mind, we exhale, throwing the air out through the mouth, forcibly, in a series of puffs, like the effort made in blowing out a candle light.

This process must be backed by faith, or a feeling of certainty that the system will be cleansed. A sacred writer omits referring to the breathing but refers to the fact that the heart must be purified by faith. In Hartman's translation of the works of Paracelsus we find this clear cut statement:

"**A Strong Faith and Imagination** are the two pillars supporting the door to the temple of magic, without which nothing can be accomplished. Imagination is the creative power of man, and it may act instinctively and without any conscious effort of the will.

"'Man has a visible and an invisible workshop. The visible one is his body, the invisible one his mind. The sun gives light, and this light is not tangible, but its heat may be felt, and if its rays are concentrated it may set a house on fire. The Imagination is a Sun in the soul of man, acting in its own sphere as the Sun of the Earth acts in that of the latter. Whenever the latter shines, germs planted in the soil grow and vegetation springs up, and the Sun of the soul acts in a similar manner and calls the forms of the soul into existence.

" 'Visible and tangible forms grow into existence from invisible elements by the power of the sunshine. Invisible vapors are attracted and collected into visible mists by the power of the Sun of the outer world, and the inner Sun of man works similar wonders.

" 'The great world is only a product of the imagination of the Universal Mind, and man is a little world of his own, that imagines, and creates by the power of imagination.

" 'If man's imagination is strong enough to penetrate into every corner of his interior world, it will be able to create things in those corners, and whatever man thinks, takes form in his soul.' "

This great man who knew man well, has thus given us much light on the powers of man, and following in the wake of his thoughts we are doubly impressed with the fact that man can, by the power of will, faith, and imagination, bring unto himself all the powers of the Universe; hence the Spirits of Electricity, Magnetism and Azothel will come to him who Wills.

Entering the Alchemic Laboratory. Having purified the heart by Faith, and with a vivid

HELPFULNESS OF UNSEEN FORCES

Imagination, one is ready to enter the workshop of mind as creator or unfolder.

First, concentrate Thought upon the **Electric Ether**, which is everywhere abundant. Mark, this is the ether that will effect the brain; it is the intellectual ether, it is cool and invigorating. **Desire** and **expect** this ether to pour into your receptive brain with power. Take a deep full breath and hold it for a long time; then exhale slowly. In mystic lore **seven** is the number of the Electric Ether, and one may take seven such Breaths; but care must be exercised, and if dizziness supervenes the exercise must cease. This Breath may be taken at any time; but the best time is at the rising of the Sun, and one should face the east. Practice on this breath until you feel a true intellectual glow.

The Magnetic Breath. This is taken very much the same as the Electric Breath, only the thought is centered upon the Love-side of life. The heart will be mostly affected. One must simply reach out for Magnetic power. Mark, the results of this Breath are warm, not cool. **Five** is the number of the Magnetic Breath, and ordinarily five breaths may be taken at one sitting. It is best taken at sunset or the full of the Moon.

The Azothic, or Spiritual Breath is the most powerful of the Breaths that man can with safety take. It is to be taken like the Magnetic Breath, only the thought is concentrated upon one's highest ideal of Spiritual power. Reach up for that wisdom that comes only from above, and he who can close up all the avenues of the senses will see God face to face. **Three** is the number of the Azothic Breath, and never more than three such Breaths should be taken at one sitting. It has the most power, when taken at noon or midnight.

LESSON VII.

The Holy Spirit—The Holy Ghost of Modern Theology—As a Myth and a Reality; Its Identity the True Secret of Jesus; Its Reception Completes Spiritual Unfoldment

The Holy Spirit! One of the most sacred appellations in the English language, yet one so little understod. Theologians of all the centuries of this era have quarrelled about it, have fought about it and have made it the cause of many divisions in the Church, and even at the present day the great ecclesiastical lights seem to be at sea with reference to its identity and its offices.

As the reception of the Holy Spirit by man is the culminating step in his complete unfoldment, its consideration is certainly in place in this concluding lecture on Self Culture.

Definition. The word **Holy** is derived from an old Anglo-Saxon word, "hal," from which came the English word "hale," from which we get our word "heal." The word really means whole or entire. Arbitrarily it has been made to mean "a complete setting apart for sacred or divine purposes." The word **Spirit** comes from the same word from which we get our word spire and spiral, which have reference to form and motion, indicating that which moves in spirals. The word having direct reference to air would seem to mean, "the movement of the air in spirals."

The word spirit is Latin and means the air, or the breath, corresponding with the Greek word, "pneuma," which in the authorized version of the New Testament is, usually, translated spirit.

According to the meaning of words we would, then, define the Holy Spirit as the "Breath of God moving in spirals."

Ghosts. This word is derived from the Anglo-Saxon word "gost," which means "a breath, a specter, something very thin, transparent, etherial." In time it came to mean "a spirit." The current use of the word differs much from the ancient use of it. Now it means a spook, an apparition, something ghostly, terrifying. It is certainly unfortunate that our learned ecclesiastics still use it as an appellation for the most lovable of all the beings in the Universe.

Modern Orthodoxy is not monotheism. It is a system of polytheistic philosophy from beginning to end. Every recognized theologian pours forth his supplications to **three Gods**—

God the Father, God the Son, and God the Holy Ghost, and still he resents with vigor the accusation that he believes in more than one God. He attempts to harmonize his polytheistic monotheism by saying: These three are one; and this gives him an opportunity to preach a lot of sermons on the **Unity of the Trinity** to the utter disgust of thinkers and the applause of the faithful.

The Philosophy of Orthodoxy is sound, we can take no exception to its monotheism nor its polytheism. It is right in assuming on one day that there are three Gods, and on the next that there is one God. We only take exceptions to its illogical and irrational attempts to prove that they say the same thing both days, and that three are one. A parallel case is found in an attempt to prove that a father, a mother and a child are one; but the absurdity requires no comment.

The Word God means only good; but it has so long been used to denote the Infinite One that it would be worse than folly to try to restrict it to the original idea underlying the word, and so we frequently make use of it in the place of the word **Aum,** the universal spirit. In this sense God is one, and monotheism is true. In one, however, there is not, and never was, and never can be, any creation, for unity is inert.

In the Unity-God there were forever the two principles of generation, the masculine and the feminine, and when the Universal Spirit would manifest, the one became two;

and the masculine Jehovah, and the feminine El Shaddi stood forth as the first manifests with all the creative potencies that were concealed from all eternity, in the one—the **Aum**; and so from the beginning of creation polytheism was true.

Jehovah is the Almighty God, the God of force; El Shaddi is the ommiscient God, the God of Intelligence, or Wisdom; so Force is masculine; Intelligence is feminine. In the activities of the masculine and the feminine, Jehovah and El Shaddi, the Logos came forth as the only begotten Son, the Love, and Jehovah became "our Father who art in heaven," and El Shaddi became, "our Mother who art in heaven," and the Logos, the eternal Christ, "our Elder Brother," and the universe recognized the trinity, God the Father, God the Mother, and God the Son.

..**The Holy Spirit** of Orthodoxy is the El Shaddi of the Hebrew theogony; is the Wisdom or Intelligence of the one God; is feminine, and is the Second person in the trinity and not the third.

The Holy Spirit, the Holy Breath, the feminine principle of the God-Head; how may she be received, and what are the advantages of such reception is the subject of this study.

The word **Wisdom** comprises the essential qualities of the Holy Spirit.

Among the wisest things that Solomon ever said was:

"My Son, get **Wisdom,** get understanding; forsake her not and she will preserve thee;

love her and she will keep thee. Wisdom is the principal thing; therefore, get Wisdom; exalt her and she will promote thee; and will bring thee to honor, when thou dost embrace her. She will give to thy head an ornament of grace; a crown of glory will she deliver to thee." Prov. 4.

Note that Solomon always refers to Wisdom as the feminine.

In Prov. 3rd Chapter, Solomon breaks forth in a sublime eulogy upon Wisdom; and this eulogy is worth committing to memory. He says:

"Happy is the man who findeth Wisdom; for the merchandise of her is better than the merchandise of silver, and the gain thereof than fine gold. She is more precious than rubies; and all the things thou canst desire are not to be compared unto her. Length of days is in her right hand; and in her left hand riches and honor. Her ways are ways of pleasantness and all her paths are peace. She is a tree of life to those who lay hold upon her, and happy is every one who retaineth her."

When you come to recognize the fact that nearly the entire Book of Proverbs is a descriptive commentary upon the Holy Spirit, you will probably read it with greater interest.

James, the Christian Apostle, refers to this same Holy Spirit when he writes: "The **Wisdom** that is from above is first pure, then peaceable, gentle, easy to be entreated, full of mercy and good fruits, without partiality and without hypocrisy." James 3:17.

The Holy Spirit is taken from the domain of incomprehensible things and the realm of uncertain and uncanny mysticism when we realize that she is **Wisdom,** pure and simple.

With this idea in mind, the parting words of Jesus to his disciples are recovered from murkiness: He said, "I have yet many things to say unto you, but ye cannot bear them now. Howbeit when she, the Spirit of Truth is come, she will guide you into all truth." John 16:12, 13.

This is Not Sacrilegious. In this rational study of the Holy Spirit we do not degrade this second person of the Sacred Trinity; but we exalt Wisdom, something that no earth-lexicographer has yet been able to define.

Wisdom is not Knowledge; it is the Great Spirit that leads the way to knowledge, a thought so well expressed by Jesus.

Wisdom is a Universal ether, one of the three Attributes of the Eternal One, and it is this ether that we receive by inspiration. This Holy Breath, or Holy Spirit is that to which Paul referred when he said, "All Scripture is given because of the in-breathing, or taking in of God;" and this gives us a hint as to the manner in which we must receive the Holy Spirit. Jesus made prominent the idea that the Holy Spirit was received by breathing; for after his resurrection it is said of him that he breathed upon his disciples and said, "Receive ye the Holy Spirit." John 20:22.

Receiving the Holy Spirit. We have had many lessons upon the true Science of the Great Breath, and we are familiar with almost numberless forms of breathing; we have learned how we may insure health by appropriate breathing; how we may become clairvoyant and clairaudient by taking in, in certain ways the Great Breath; and we know of the advantages of these Breaths in psychic and the lower trend of Spiritual unfoldment, but we now come to a place where methods seem like idle talk.

Orientalists have told us of a Breath that is too high to be taken by carnal beings with safety, and we know that there is such a Breath, and that it opens up the door to the very presence-chamber of God, and still it pales into insignificance when we come to stand in the presence of the Spirit. This is the plane of the Breathless Breath, the voiceless Voice, the soundless sound; a place that cannot be entered until one has, by ages of effort in self control and self purification, brought himself in rapport with the Great Over Soul. Here one breathes, but it is unconscious breathing; one hears, but it is unconscious hearing; one sees, but it is unconscious seeing; one feels, but it is unconscious feelings; one knows, but it is unconscious knowing, for he has "come unto the Mount Sion, and unto the city of the living God, the heavenly Jersualem, and to an innumerable company of angels, to the general assembly, and church of the first born, which are written in heaven, and to God, the Judge of all, and to the spirits of just men made perfect." Here he is wholly absorbed by the ethers of Divine Wisdom; fully baptised in the Spirit.

The Spiritual Mind, or that which is recognized in Hindu Philosophy as the Sixth Principle of man, is here unfolded. You cannot breath it in; it is **Transmutation;** it is the man himself spiritualized. Paul referred to this transmutation when he wrote to the Corinthians, "Behold, I show you a mystery; we shall not all sleep, but we shall all be changed; this corruptible must put on incorruption."

This is the plane of spiritual consciousness; it is attained by a godly life. A Hindu teacher once said, "As a man's spiritual consciousness begins to unfold, he begins to have an abiding sense of the reality of the existence of the Supreme Power, and, growing along with it, he finds the sense of Human Brotherhood—of human relationship—gradually coming into consciousness. He does not get these things from his Instinctive mind, nor does his Intellect make him feel them." **The Spiritual Mind** is the source of the inspiration which certain Poets, Painters, Sculptors, Writers, Preachers, Orators and others have received in all times, and which they receive today. This is the source from which the seer (spiritual) obtains his visions; the prophet his foresight. Many have concentrated themselves upon high ideals in their work, and have received rare knowledge from this source, and have attributed it to beings of another world—from angels, spirits and from God himself, when all came from within; it was the voice of their higher self speaking to them.

"When man learns of the existence of his Spiritual Mind, and begins to recognize its promptings and leadings, he strengthens his bond of communication with it, and consequently receives light of a greater brilliancy. When we learn to **trust** the Spirit, it responds by sending us more frequent flashes of illumination and enlightenment. As one unfolds in spiritual consciousness he relies more on this Inner voice, and is able to distinguish it from impulses from the lower planes of the mind. Many of us have learned to know the reality of being "led by the Spirit."

Proofs of Spiritual Consciousness are called for by the disciples every day. How may one recognize the promptings of the Spirit? An Occult teacher of considerable power has said something that will help to answer this question. He said:

"With many, spiritual mind unfolds gradually and slowly, and while one may feel a steady increase of spiritual knowledge and consciousness, he may not have experienced any marked or startling change. Others have had moments of what is known as 'Illumination,' when they seem lifted almost out of their normal state, and where they seem to pass into a higher plane of consciousness or being, which left them more advanced than before, although they could not carry back into consciousness a clear recollection of what they had experienced, while in that exalted state of mind. These experiences have come to many persons in different forms and degrees under all forms of religious beliefs. * * * *

"These experiences vary according to the degree of unfoldment and previous training; but certain characteristics are common to all. The most common feeling is that of possessing almost complete knowledge of all things—almost Omniscience. This feeling exists only for a moment, and leaves one at first in an agony of regret over what he has seen and lost.

"Another feeling commonly experienced is that of a certainty of immortality—a sense of actual being, and the certainty of having always been, and of being destined to always be.

"Another feeling is the total slipping away of all fear, and the acquirement of a feeling of certainty, trust and confidence, which is beyond the comprehension of those who have never experienced it.

"Then a feeling of love sweeps over one—a love which takes in all life, from those near to one in the flesh to those at the farthest parts of the Universe; from those whom we hold as pure and holy, to those whom the world regards as vile and utterly unworthy. All feelings of self-righteousness and condemnation seem to slip away, and one's love, like the light of the Sun, falls upon all alike,

THE HOLY SPIRIT

irrespective of their degree of development or goodness.'"

The Rapport. Such experience is what is with propriety called the Rapport. In its fullness it may not come to a person more than once in a lifetime, but when it does come it leaves an impression that cannot be forgotten. We always remember that time with unbounded joy. One of the early Christian fathers referred to such an experience as a glimpse of heaven; he said, "In all of my life I have experienced it once; a brother minister has experienced it twice, but the bishop has never been blessed even once with it." An Occult historian says:

"From the writings of the ancient philosophers of all races, from the songs of the great poets of all peoples, from the preachings of the prophets of all religions and times we can gather traces of this Illumination which has come to them—this unfoldment of the Spiritual Consciousness. One has told of it in one way, the other in another way; but all tell practically the same story. It is the song of the soul, which when once heard is never forgotten. Though it be sounded by the crude instruments of the semi-barbarous races, or the finished instrument of the talented musician of today, its strains are plainly recognized. From old Egypt comes the song; from India in all ages; from ancient Greece and Rome; from the early Christian Saint; from the Quaker Friend; from the Catholic monasteries; from Mohammedan mosque; from the Chinese philosopher; from the legends of Hiawatha, the American Indian hero-prophet—it is always the same strain, and it is swelling louder and louder, as many more are taking it up and adding their voices or the sound of their instruments to the grand chorus."

Our own Walt Whitman must have had snatches of this ecstacy, for once he said:

"As in a swoon, one instant,
Another sun, ineffable, full dazzles me,
And all the orbs I knew, and brighter, unknown, orbs,
One instant of the future land, Heaven's land."

And then the great soul comes to himself and exclaims:

"I cannot be awake, for nothing looks to me as it did before;
Or else I am awake for the first time, and all before has been a mean sleep."

Of the ecstacy of one moment of divine Illumination tongue cannot tell. Even the versatile Whitman was forced to say:

"When I try to tell the best I find, I cannot;
My tongue is ineffectual on its pivot;
My breath will not be obedient to its organs;
I become a dumb man!"

Illumination! Inexplicable word. The goal is high, but not too high for human possibilities; but it cannot be reached by any of the clumsily made machines of man. You cannot attain it by forms and ceremonies, by **ablutions** and sacrifices; it is the culmination of nothing but **A Holy Life**.

The Aquarian Gospel of Jesus the Christ

"The Most Wonderful Book of the Ages"

Transcribed from the Book of God's Remembrance,
the Akashic Records.

By LEVI.

From whence came the information which enabled Levi to write this book? This is a most difficult question to answer for the comprehension of people not familiar with spiritual law, but those who have entered into Spiritual Consciousness will comprehend.

A Book of Remembrance is forever kept in the secret pavilion of God where every sound, color, word and thought is registered. Malachi wrote: "They that feared the Lord spake often one to another and the Lord hearkened and heard; and a book of Remembrance was written before him." Mal. 3:16.

Oriental scholars call this Book of Remembrance, "Akashic Records," and recognize the fact that men do attain unto such heights of spiritual consciousness that they may at will enter into these record chambers and transcribe and take back to men whatever is for the good of men. By the efforts of a most strenuous life, yea, of lives, Levi was qualified to enter these galleries and read these records, and he brought to men this volume—The Aquarian Gospel of Jesus the Christ.

Levi's work stands unimpeachable. The character of the translated texts and lessons bear the stamp of Jesus, the Christ; for no man, except the world's greatest master, could have touched the high chords and divine wisdom which these messages breathe forth.

Choice of Stiff or Flexible Cloth Binding, Price $2.00.
E. S. Dowling, Publisher, 503 S. Figueroa St., Los Angeles, Cal.

OPINIONS OF COMPETENT REVIEWERS

Julia Seton Sears, M. D. Founder of the New Thought Church and School in America and England, writes:

"The outer world of higher metaphysics has lost a master and the inner spiritual kingdoms of life have gained a prophet—'Levi, the Seer,' no longer contacts this outer rim of living, but from the plane of higher consciousness his messages will forever reach backward to those who are waiting for his words.

"He came and went under his own divine law; lived his hours upon the earth; brought his message and passed on; always the 'elder brother' of the race, beckoning them onward up the path of life.

"He was one of those rare messengers who throughout the centuries have come out upon the race path to let the light of life shine more clearly, and we know that those who follow the call of this illumined soul can not walk in darkness but they have ever the light of life.

"From the upper spiritual realms his glorified consciousness still leads on and the messages he left will stand for centuries as a benediction for those who are seeking the deeper spiritual illumination of life.

"Our hearts grieve with the emptiness of a great human loss, for on the path of life this man of God was a comforter, a friend and a guide, but knowing the endless chain of life, we see our loss as his eternal gain and we feel with all the conviction of our deeper understanding there is no parting, death is only the inside of Life itself, and consciousness answers to consciousness throughout all space.

"He was the translator of a higher divine vision, a messenger of the true Gods, and on the rock of the divine at-one-ment, God in unity with man, he built his temple, and throughout all the centuries of the new civilization millions of hearts will worship at this true shrine.

"Centuries may come and go, but the immortal message of Levi, the prophet, transcriber of the Sacred records and great human revelator will burn like a glorious beacon light, shining more and more upon the pathway of the race, leading ever onward to life's perfect way."

James M. Peebles, M. A., M. D., Ph. D., whose name is a household word in thousands of homes, writes:

"The history of Jesus the Christ, the central figure of the world's most enlightened nations, recorded by the Evangelists, and elaborated, somewhat, in the Pauline Epistles, is in this wonderful work—The Aquarian Gospel of Jesus the Christ— filled out, or furthered and exemplified in the teachings, the spiritual doings and the extensive travels of the Nazarene in Egypt, Persia, India and other countries.

"The Universe knows no loss. The lives of all great souls are recorded in eternity. This was the case of the man Jesus, the Christ, and the mystic LEVI, the soul of candor and spirituality, through concentrations, meditations and spiritual unfoldings was, like Paul of old, intromitted into the fields of Paradise, or unto those other spheres of immortality, where he transcribed and transmitted to earth, the beautiful, inspiring and uplifting teachings of this Aquarian Gospel. There was no miracle in this, in the old sense of that word, but a dispensation on the part of the gods to give us clearer views, and more of the marvelous realities that characterized the life of the Nazarene."

W. J. Colville, world-renowned lecturer, writes:

"Among the many truly remarkable and occasionally epoch-making books which have recently issued from the teeming press we know of no one quite so remarkable in its peculiar line as the Aquarian Gospel, which undertakes to give an account of the life of Jesus much ampler than any accepted version of the New Testament furnishes. Though a great deal of this marvelous narrative follows rather closely along familiar lines there are many instances where it shows a wide departure, chiefly by introducing matter of extreme interest noticeably absent from the well known gospels. The specially unique matter concerns the life of Jesus during the 17 or 18 years intervening between his appearance in the Temple at Jerusalem when twelve or thirteen years of age and his public appearance in Palestine as a teacher and healer of multitudes at the age of 30.

"Among a great many intensely interesting and highly fascinating narratives with which the work abounds, the section describing the Council of the World's Seven Sages is certainly one of the most absorbing. Into the midst of this august assemblage Jesus introduces words of wisdom which all alike can accept and follow, for he speaks of universal truth, adapted to all alike, regardless of creed or nationality, and also regardless of age or condition. As we continue the narrative and proceed to consider the several consecutive stages which led to Jesus becoming the great Master he eventually became, we find that he underwent every trial and temptation incidental to human progress; the book, therefore, is extremely valuable from a more than simply historical standpoint, for it clearly introduces to our notice the steps in initiation which lead to ultimate triumph over all earthly limitations. The wonderful Akashic records, from which this amazing narrative has been secured, are open to the scrutinizing vision of all who have truly developed the gifts of seership, but few are they in whom this vision is as yet largely unfolded, though we may expect it to develop as the race progresses."

Alfred Tomson, Secretary National New Thought Alliance, regarding the Aquarian Gospel of Jesus the Christ, says:

"I have been deeply impressed with its value as a helpful and useful book.

"I am glad to say that I accept this Gospel as the gift of a great soul—a gift from the Divine to the world—a message measuring out a pure and sweet gospel to mankind, a simple wholesome teaching inspiring a broader vision to the beholden eyes of men.

"It is a Seer's vision and spoken with a prophet's voice, proclaiming in accents sweet and clear the old-new story of truth and love, the story of mundane and cosmic life, of God and man —the Divine Unity—the Eternal Parallel, reigning throughout the universe.

"It is, to me, a very great pleasure in my ministry to speak as often as I can from this Aquarian Scripture, and to urge myself and all men to live up to its lofty and beautiful teachings.

"I therefore sincerely commend the Aquarian Gospel to all students of the higher life in the here and now."

THIRD EDITION of The Aquarian Gospel is now upon the market. Choice of Stiff or Flexible Cloth Binding, Price $2.00.

Address all orders to

E. S. DOWLING   Los Angeles, Cal.